From Here To There

A Journey In Love Poems and Letters

I0162501

Alexander Michaels

Kingsway Publishing

London, Miami

Self Development .Org

www.selfdevelopment.org

Published By

Kingsway Publishing

318 Indian Trace, Suite 527,

Weston Florida 33326

ISBN: 978-0-9542470-6-5

Printed in the United States of America

About The Author

Alexander Michaels is the author of self-development and wealth creation books and courses. He is the author of the "Broke To Millionaire In 90 Days" course and "Relationship Marketing" book as well as the "Secrets of Self-Mastery" and "From Fear To Courage" books and courses. He is an insightful speaker and consultant to businesses that wish to develop the full potential of their staff and resources. He may be reached by email at authors@selfdevelopment.org

Dedication

I dedicate this book to the loving memories of my mother and my father.

Acknowledgements

I would like to thank my brother Sylvester for being everything that anyone could want in a brother. I would like to thank every woman that has been a part of my life starting from my mother, my sisters to my friends and associates and especially my daughter Jasmine. They have surely helped me become more of who I am than I would have been otherwise.

CONTENTS   Page

Contents

Contents

Contents

Introduction

"From Here To There" *A Journey In Love Poems and Letters* is a very personal collection of poems and letters I have written over the years. It covers a personal journey spanning a range of emotions from happiness to sadness and back to happiness, from love to un-love, and from unloved to loved. A personal journey that I am sure will resonate with many readers of this work.

So understand that this is not just a book of poems full of sugar and honey. It is a book that reflects the true range of feelings that I have experienced and that I know most people including you also experience.

It reflects real life feelings.

For how can you learn how to be happy, when you do not know when or what has made you unhappy?

And how can you appreciate true happiness, when you have not experienced true unhappiness?

One is a reflection of the other. And it is in seeing and admitting the existence of both sides of the reflection, that we can make a conscious effort to decide which part we want to live and which part must remain simply, a reflection.

Some of the letters are letters that I have written to myself and want to share with you. And others are letters that I have written because the words came to me and I simply had to write them down. Maybe they are words that you can relate to. One of the letters was from a vision I received regarding a friend of mine. She was going through some life-changing experiences at the time and one day I woke up with these words that seemed to be a message for her. I wrote the vision down and sent it to her. She has kindly allowed me to include it in this work and insisted that I left it intact without editing.

This is how I experience these "letters" sometimes:

I wake up and realize that I have just had a lengthy conversation within me

And realize that I must get it on paper and out from inside of me.

For it is in reading the words from when sleeping that my subconscious has just sent to me,

that I fully realize the person that I am or should want to be

I have used classic paintings to represent and compliment some of the poems. I have always been a lover of paintings and somehow feel that by using paintings from the past it reinforces the fact that our personal life-love stories, however beautiful or intense, have been experienced similarly by others in the past and that such experiences are a common factor in the human story from time immemorial. Using paintings from times of old reaffirms the timelessness of love and poetry.

We are unique in our feelings and yet we are all quite similar. Perhaps we can look at the experiences of those that have gone before us to understand that we are not alone, and that our happiness and unhappiness, love and regrets, and hope and faith have already been experienced by others and will no doubt continue to be experienced in the future.

Knowing that our time here is temporary but that our emotions have been experienced by others in the past and can be manifested in the future, we may decide to be more selective about what we feel and lean more on the side of hope and love.

This commonality amongst us, be we lovers or just friends, can be a source of great comfort and love during times of emotional or spiritual challenges. These are my thoughts in poems and letters. This is how I see things.

Alexander Michaels

Alexander Michaels

Find Me

*I was riding on my black stallion, on a quite
morning, on the beautiful soft sands of a golden
beach.*

*Then I heard the sound of a mermaid singing, her
song was so beautiful that it sent my heart singing.*

*So I rode towards the sound, and as I got closer
my steed moved faster.*

*Then I saw the mermaid and realized that it was
you.*

*I slowed down as I saw that you had company.
You were smiling and seemed so happy.*

*You smiled at me and I smiled back, then to your
conversations and company you went back.*

*So I turned back because I saw that you were OK
and occupied. But my steed would not let me and
he turned towards you and rushed me towards
you.*

Alexander Michaels

And as I got closer I saw your smile closer,
and as I saw your smile closer I saw that you
wanted me closer.

You were smiling and crying at the same time, for
the company was not the best company.

Faster and faster my steed galloped towards you,
it's eyes focused and it's nostrils blasting jets of
steam against the cold morning air.

And now I knew what my steed was telling me,
it was time to rescue a mermaid who had called
and sung to me.

So my sword I pulled out and pointed ahead of
me,
ready to lay down my life for this woman that was
in front of me.

I saw your aura beginning to crumble under the
oppressive energy of the company.
So I swung left and right to destroy the
undeserved company.

The fight was hard and many times I thought I
would not prevail.
But one look in your eyes was enough to push me,
for complete victory I knew that I must avail.

*For your look had now changed to a look of hope
at last
A hope long desired and a hope your heart almost
had lost.*

*Through morning, noon and night the battle raged
on.
Until I prevailed with my clothes all torn and my
mind totally worn.*

*I ran to you as your aura shield collapsed, and
picked you up just before you hit the ground. You
looked into my eyes and whispered:*

**"You have found me",
"long has your princess sung to you and now
you have found me"**

*Your eyes closed and I thought I might have lost
you.
So gently I kissed your lips as my tears fell on you.*

*For eternity it seemed with you in my arms I stood
there,
my arms straining but I would not put you down
there.*

*What is that I see, a precious glow coming from
your heart. And looking closer I notice your heart
beginning to beat ever so gently.*

Then the glow from my body was drawn by you,
as it moved towards yours and together they
became joined into one whole.

That was when your eyes slowly opened and you
looked into my mine and whispered again:

"Long have I waited and no other has
satiated".
"Darling where were you when I almost
fainted?"

"I did not give up, I prayed that you would find
me".
"And now my spirit is high up, because my

prince you have found me".

Where have You Been

So where have you been?

When I searched for you in the pouring rain

I search for you in the crowded streets,

Like trying to find the brightest amongst the stars

But you must have been hiding,

Afraid of pain and hurt that in your life has caused
you strain

I search for words to send you,

But my heart is beginning to fail me

So now you have come home again,

You there standing in the door wet from the rain

In your teary eyes I can see all the pain,

And I say come in and let true love upon you rain

You Asked Me Why

You asked me why I chose you,
And to this choice can I stand firm and true

It was no accident that you searched and found
me,
For it was your love search that led a path to me

This magic connection we have is just pure
magnetic,
And the feeling that we share is a trust that's
simply fantastic

You asked me why I chose you,
Was it your smile that pulled me to you?

I say what true man that sees a bright diamond on
a black sandy beach,
Would ignore it and ride by on his white steed and
for it not reach

Alexander Michaels

After listening to your sweet and sultry voice,
I knew to love one like you I would have but no
choice

For know I that tis better to travel a 1,000 miles for
such a beautiful one,
Than to shuffle a few feet for mediocrity and regret
in the long run

Surely you know I saw you in a dream before we
met,
That was why I knew I must catch you in my love
net

For to my heart your soul has been singing,
And now your voice sets my body tingling

Now that your soul has so gently touched mine,
I can see how together our future will surely shine

For I thought I did not need anything from you,
But now I know I must have everything in you

And I though I did not want anything from you,
But now I know I cannot live without everything
from you

You asked me why I chose you,
And I answer: It was always you, it is you, and it

will always be you

I still Love You

I still love you
Even when you are angry

I still love you
Even when you are sad

I still love you
When you first wake up and all grumpy

I still love you
As I watch you sleeping even like a baby

I still love you
Without makeup and your hair all messed up

I still love you
When you're dressed to take on the world and
universe

And why do I still love you so?
Because I just do, and you are a now a part of me

Now That I Have

Tasted You

Now that I have tasted you,
Why would I let you go away?

Now that I have tasted you,
Why do you push me away?

Your words may push me away,
But your heart calls and to you I sway

Out of respect I listen to your words,
But out of love I listen to your heart

Of course I am strong and can live without you,
But what good is that without your love that is
sweet and true?

Now that I have tasted you,
Will you stop pushing me away?

Now that I have tasted you,
Will you let me truly love and care for you?

Alexander Michaels

So Here I Am

So here I am,
And I wonder where you are

You asked me to search for you,
And to your request I have been true

You said I must meet you by the sea under the
moonlight,
And I was surely there searching in vain for your
bright light

You say that many have courted you,
But I say I know that this is nothing new

You say that many have called and run to you,
But your heart was not moved and none has truly
sung to you

And you ask why should your heart want and open
up for me,
And I reply, truly as there is only one heaven and
earth, you will find no other like me

Alexander Michaels

For tis true that many have called and run to you,
But only I will truly listen and move heaven and
earth for you

For what your heart desires many will seek but not
many will find,
But I have the gift to unlock your heart, a heart that
is special and only one of a kind

It Takes Courage

It takes courage to decide who you want to be

*It takes courage to overcome the unhelpful actions
of those that would stop you from becoming who
you want to be*

*It takes courage to take the first steps towards
becoming who you want to be.*

*It takes courage to continue in the face of difficult
challenges and stay true to who you want to be.*

*But it takes the greatest courage to accept others
for who they want to be*

*And to realize that you do not loose any of yourself
but rather gain if you let them be*

*Take courage and give some of who you are in
order that others can become more of who and
what they want to be.*

*For it is in giving more of who you are,
that you truly become more of who you should
want to be*

Alexander Michaels

I Wake Up To Me

*Sometimes I wake up and realize that I have just
had a lengthy conversation within me*

*And realize that I must get it on paper and out
from inside of me.*

*For it is in reading the words from when sleeping
that my subconscious has just sent to me,*

*that I fully realize the person that I am or should
want to be*

......

The next poem, "I Just Wondered If..." I wrote one day when I was wondering what makes a person differentiate and choose another. What I concluded was that really no two people are exactly the same. And in fact if you were to meet two people that appear to be exactly the same and by chance fall in love with one, then the mere act of you falling in love with that one will make him or her different from the other. You may suddenly see qualities in them that you did not know existed previously. Qualities that do not now existed in the other.

So what lovers sometimes forget until it is too late is that what made them *unique* was partially the love that existed between them. When that love is diminished then the uniqueness sometimes diminishes too. Then they start searching for someone unique again.

Alexander Michaels

I just wondered if...

The world is full of beautiful women,
This I know very well

The world is overflowing with creative and
accomplished women,
This I cannot deny

The world is truly blessed with millions or loving
and caring women,
This has made the world a better place for all

The world is more vibrant because of the energy
of passionate women,
This I must have for myself

But the world only has one woman with the most
exquisite combination of beauty, intelligence and
accomplishments, loving and caring, and passion
without boundaries that many search for

And I wondered today if that woman could
possibly be you.

What Does He Want

He wants an intelligent woman that he can have meaningful conversations with about different things

A caring and loving woman that is not afraid to completely love the man in her life

A woman that is more reserved than loud, but still vibrant and lively

A sensual woman

A woman that loves to be loved

A woman that is comfortable in jeans and t-shirt but also truly enjoys dressing up elegantly

A woman that cares about the needs of those less fortunate than herself or family and who shows it in action and deed, not just words.

A woman that is fully supportive of her man and family just as he would be supportive of her

A confident woman that does not need him but does want him.

Basically, the lady of his dreams would be simply a genuine and nice lady

That is what he wants and that is all he desires

You Ask If I Like Your Pictures

You ask me if I like your pictures,
as I sit and ponder about our futures

You smile at me through your pictures,
And I think you are a woman that nurtures

How can I resist you, and how should I fight?
As your pictures into my soul they bring light

How many ways should I like you?
Enjoy the aura that's all around you

You legs I want wrapped around me,
As we make passionate love you and me

Alexander Michaels

Your arms draped over my shoulders,
And our eyes stare at each other with wonder

You breast pressing against me through your shirt
As I think with me you want to flirt

My hands squeezing tightly your rear-side,
Oh I pray tonight I'll have you by the fireside

Then I say this lady she loves me,
And I say I will lay with her and keep her for me

Yes I Must Talk To You

Yes, I must talk to you. The picture in your letter looking straight into my eyes and hypnotizing me.

You have taken the time to say more about yourself than most people would do. And what I see and read indicates to me that you are no ordinary one. You are a thinker, you have soul and you are not afraid to show it.

It takes courage to ask for love and to allow oneself to be loved. Life is a risk. Anything worthwhile includes some element of risk, and asking for love exposes one to risk.

But not asking for love almost guarantees failure in one of life's most precious and honorable goals.

I was glad, when I read your letter, that you appear to be a person that is confident in their identity, and yet is not afraid to enjoy the pleasures of being a beautiful and loveable being. You appear to be the kind of person that most would truly treasure, because it is clear that when you ask for love you are willing and ready to receive it. What great man could say no to a lady such as you? What true gentleman can say no to a princess who is looking for a prince. For how can a prince become all that he can be, if he does not have a princess to complete him and make him more than he has been?

You have nothing to prove, but you have much coming to you. You are excited about life and will not accept anything less than living my life to the full, and with unabashed passion with the one that will complete your soul.

......

The poem "Your call To Me" is basically a description of the way couples try to show what they perceive to be their most attractive qualities to each other when first courting. The complex act of human courtship sometimes reminds me of the way birds call to each other and sometimes use songs and posturing to attract the most suitable partner. We are not so different, I don't think, from the birds.

Alexander Michaels

Your Call To Me

A thousand words I will send to you,
Because a thousand miles cannot stand between
me and you

What I hear is what your words tell me,
But what I feel is what your expressions show me

The call of your smile I cannot ignore,
When my soul your smile has called to the fore

You say you are sweet,
Your smile I know will drive suitors to your feet

You say you are kind,
Must be true because to me you look like one of a
kind

You say you are compassionate,
To my soul that part of you truly resonates

You proclaim to the world that you are honest,
How can anyone ignore that you are earnest?

But you want me to know you are genuine,
As true and delicate as a rare gentle-wine

Alexander Michaels

So let me make you mine - for as long as the sun shines,
For I tell you the truth - another love like mine you will never find

......

The next poem, "There Can Only Be One", was actually a section from a long dream that I had one day. It was part of an epic story, an adventure, that was quite fun and that felt like a movie. I wrote part of it down as a poem but the rest I have long since forgotten.

Alexander Michaels

There Can Only Be One

Truly I tell you, there is no maiden as fine as thee. Tis possible that some other fair maiden might overhear me as I profess my love for thee, but you are my only intended audience. Give me thine name now and I will write a poem for thee that will prove that your heart is my one and only intention.

Twas a dark night when I first saw your outline, from your window in the king's castle as I was riding by on my black stallion. You were singing a song so beautiful that I profess I at first thought it must have been an angel singing. It was a song of longing, of passion, of a calling for a prince to rescue you. I was mesmerized, my steed froze in step and we both looked up at your window. But you did not see us. So lonely and heartbroken was your song.

Since that day I have vowed that I will find thee and make thee mine. And now I have discovered thee here. Truly I tell you this, no other maiden has captured my heart as much as ye has from that single moment.

*What can I do to prove to thee that there cannot
be any other?
What can I do to show that thine eyes are like
sweet nectar without which my soul will surely die?*

*What can I say to prove to thee that there is only
one prince that truly deserves thee; one prince
that ye truly deserve; one prince that will protect
and care for thee come what may; one prince that
has searched heaven and earth for thee?*

What, pray tell, must I do to make thee mine?

*For I tell you this, in my mind you are a princess,
and I must make thee mine. I have a kingdom that
I must conquer, and the only thing missing would
be a princess by my side to become my queen?
Do you think you can ever become my maiden, my
princess, my queen?*

*I have found thee. Faith has brought thee to me. I
am ready to carry thee away on my black steed. I
am building a new castle for thee and a new life
for thee. A life of passion, a life of power, a life of
sweet pleasures, and a life of true love.*

*Our new kingdom awaits thee. Come princess,
now is your time, now is our time…*

I Saw You In A Magazine

I saw your face on the cover of a magazine
I was mesmerized and could not stop gazing

I wonder what you are doing, this lovely woman,
that has graced this page and confused so many
men

I wonder how many hearts you will break along the
way,
without even knowing that men have fallen for you
along the way

Did you know your smile has the power to melt the
iciest-coldest hearts?
Did you know that your smile has the power to
cool the hottest untamed hearts?

I wonder if we'll ever meet, this beautiful woman,
that has brightened this magazine and confused
so many men.

Alexander Michaels

The First Time We Met

How can I forget,
the first time we met

You looked so sweet,
I was pulled into your net

It took me a while,
to get you to smile

But when you did smile,
it gave me the will

The courage to ask,
if you would be mine,

And you replied yes,
until the end of time.

She Smiles

She smiles,
and the world brightens up

She cries
and it causes the rain to drop

She laughs
and the flowers open up

She worries,
and everyone looks fed up

That is the power your spirit has
To bring things down or raise them to the stars

That is the power your love has
To make me laugh or bring me to tears

It is a power I know you will use cautiously
Now that I have asked for your hand formally

It is a power you must use with great gentleness
To protect the love I give you with great eagerness

It Took A Dream

I woke up crying
Felt as if my heart was simply dying

Tears running down my face
My heart beating at an uncontrollable pace

So tightly you held onto me
As you wondered and looked straight up at me

Your eyes seeing through to the soul of me
Still I cried because the pain was so deep inside of
me

Tis only a nightmare, you say
Please stop crying, I pray

Yes, only a nightmare I sobbed
So terrible because of your presence I was almost
robbed

No, I cannot remember what it was that almost
happened
But it has caused my heart to become fully opened

It took an unwanted dream, an undesired dream
For me to realize that we are together an
inseparable team

I did not know how much I needed you
And I did not know how much I would miss you

I did not know how much you were a part of me
And I did not know much your love really meant to
me

My angel it took an unwanted dream to open my
eyes
To the bond that between us ties

Now as I look into your beautiful gentle eyes
I realize my love for you will never die

Calling Kari

Someone called your name, Kari
But you did not listen; still it felt so eerie

Someone called your name, Kari
But you did not listen; yet your eyes got so teary

Gently it whispered your name, Kari
And your soul and body heard it, so clearly

Your senses came alive, so strangely
You felt your body shiver, your senses all so tingly

That voice, it was so familiar
Like someone you knew, so similar

Come home to whom you are, it whispered
Come home to who I am, it inspired

Said it, wipe away the tears from your face
And all the fears and sadness, from your life you
must erase

There is no one in my eyes, none more perfect
than you

Alexander Michaels

*Please take the words I give you, in your heart
know that they are true*

*For all that has happened in your life, all that has
transpired
Has had to be, and now you must be inspired*

*For tis your time to live, your time to see
That your future can be open, as vast as the
beautiful sea*

*And it smiled; know you now the voice you hear?
And it soothed; know you now that it is someone
to you so near?*

*It is I, Kari
I am you, Kari*

*Throw away the fears
Wipe away the tears*

*Now come home to me Kari,
Please come home to us, Kari*

For Better Or Worse

We said for better or worse
When we said "I do" as we became one

We knew that nothing could separate us, no force
On this planet could break the loyal bond that
made us one

But now I sit and wonder what went wrong
With a love so pure and hopes so strong

Why am I here alone wondering were the love has
gone
When I know to another's heart your love you've
sworn

A new love I know I'll find, one more true
Still I wonder if you truly cared when you said to
me "I do"

The Colors I See

White is the color of the sands

Blue is the color of the sea

Orange is the color of the sun

And gold is the color of the ring I hold

As I sit alone on the crowded beach

Without your love that has now gone out of reach

I realize that the only color that matters to me now

Is the dark grey color you lost love has cast on my heart now

I Was Once Happy

I was once the happy one
With smiles that shone and brightened everyone

I was once the happy one
With confidence that showed I felt like I sat on a
throne

I was once the happy one
With a future so sure and a spirit that shone

Yes I was once the happy one
When I had you beside me before my heart was
torn

I Am Not Sad

No I am not sad
Even though you see tears flow down my face

Of course I am not sad
Even though I walk with my shoulders drooped
and head looking down

It is not being sad
That has stopped me from caring about what
happens today or tomorrow

No I am not sad, I am not sad, I am not sad

I am just not happy
Because since you have moved on
I have simply forgotten how it was to be happy

I Must Move On

You have gone from my life
And the pain of your departure is still ripe

Why is it so hard to forget your love still
Though many have tried and yet I am not fulfilled

I can still feel your presence every time I go there
To the place we first met and discovered love
that's so rare.

I know I must move on and live life anew
And find a new love so that my spirits I can renew

But my heart yearns for the times we had
For memories so dear and yet painful to have

I must forget you, and to pain say adieu
And find a true love that will help me live life anew

But You Did Not Tell Me

But you not did tell me
That you had another

You did not warn me
I would have to share you with some other

Would not have mattered
If I did not care for you

Would not have bothered
If my love had not grown for you

Why did you not tell me
That you were loved by another

Now there's no choice for me
Because you've become my lover

Just One Kiss

Just one kiss
And my life's in bliss

My heart feels light
Everything seems bright

A constant smile on my face
The world now I can face

All my worries are gone
And all of life seems fun

But all it took from you
Was just one kiss

Why Do I love You So?

But why do I love you so
Could it be the beautiful shape of your eyes that
melt me so

And why do I crave you so
Could it be the softness of your skin that turns me
on so

How is it your presence makes my heart beat so
Could it be the way you walk and glide across the
floor so

How can my love for you take over my body so
Because I know the way you love me none has
ever loved me so

For Eternity

Eternity is how long this love will last
I know it because it started strong and moved so
fast

Forever in my arms I will hold you no matter what
test
Life brings to us in our journey through this love
quest

It is true that our physical bodies one day will
perish
And all we see here will one day vanish

But our love will hold and will never diminish
Though space and time stops and all else is
finished

Love Is A Double Edged Sword

Love is a double-edged sword

It can take you to the highest levels of ecstasy

And it can drop you into the deepest levels of despair

It can expand your mind and release all your fantasies

And it can shrink your self-confidence and prove that the world is just not fair

It can make you risk life and limb for ones you love and care for

And it can make you into a coward unable to face challenges or move on

Love is a double-edged sword and this I know

But I also know without love life is not worth living

Someone

Someone to love me, that's all I want

Someone to cherish me, that's all I crave

Someone I fancy, that's all I desire

Someone to hold me, that's all I need

Someone to thrill me, that's all I long for

Someone to kiss me, that's all I dream for

Someone to call my own, that's all I yearn for

Someone like you, that's all I pray for

I Dreamt I found A Love

I dreamt found a love so sweet and so right
That my heart felt so light and happy that night

I dreamt that when I held you the world stood still
As we kissed and made love on top of that hill

I dreamt that your love had revitalized my soul
And transformed me from my heart to my sole

I dreamt that your smile had set my heart on fire
And now I go forward in life and do not tire

I dreamt that I held you in my arms in comfort as
you slept
And then I wake up as your breath on my face I
felt

For all the moments I just dream with you and me,
Were simply moments, recollections of our times
together and your love for me

Alexander Michaels

In God We Trust

*In god we trust
That is what it said on the coin I just picked up*

*I think back to my hopes and desires
When we first met and our love lit up*

*That day when we stood by the water fountain
And made a wish so pure before tossing that coin
into that fountain*

*A wish that our love would grow and last forever
That we would make love and dance to love songs
together*

*We looked into each other's eyes there was such
trust
That we knew that nothing could come between
and separate us*

*So now I look at the coin in my hand and just
wonder
How lucky I have been to have my wishes come
true as my heart for you grows fonder*

How Can I Live Without You

How can I live without you by my side

How can I breath, when the source of my life is no longer there

How can I continue to stand, when my strength has departed me

How can I smile, when my joy is no longer here

How can I sing, when I know you will not hear me

How can I love, when I know you're not here to receive it

How can I continue to live, without you by my side

I cannot live without you by my side

You Are The Best

You are the best
That I have ever known

Simply the best
In the way you showed me love

Effortlessly the best
In the way I see you care for others

Spiritually the best
In the way our souls connect together

Annoyingly the best
In the way you make me laugh even when mad at
you

Sensually the best
In the way you showed passion as we made love

Baby you are simply the best
That I have ever known

So Easy To Say

"I love you" is so easy to say

The words just roll out easily without thought, care or effort

I love you is such a powerful thing to say

For the impact it can have on the person who has just heard it

I love you should only be so easy to say

If you are ready to give your love, your life, and your soul to the person you say it to

Why Should I care

Why should I care
For one that hurts me so

Why should I care
For a love that has me crying

Why should I care
When you leave after promising to stay

Why should I care
Oh why should I care

Because I love you
That is why I can not help but care

Do This One Thing

Take the lead, and show the world what you're
made of

Grab the bull by the horns, and show the man how
courageous you are

Stand in front of the line and be counted, for all to
see that you have honor and will do your duty

When all is this is done, and you return home to
your sweet heart

To the one that truly loves you for who you are
and not what you prove

Can you do this one simple thing
I implore and beg of you

Grab her by the waist and pull her to you
And with great courage tell her simply "I love you"

Say You Are Sorry

When you have hurt your loved one
You may feel defensive though their heart you
have torn

You may not know what to say so you say nothing
Though in your heart you know you must do
something

Or you may think of when your heart was broken
too
Can this justify the pain just caused them by you

You may wonder if you can ever repair or make
this love stronger
If it is too late to try to rebuild you think and
wonder

When you have hurt your loved one there is but
one thing to do
Just say you are sorry and that you love them true
and true

Alexander Michaels

No One Loves You Like Me

No one is going to love you the way I love you

No mater what jewelry or gift they may buy and
give to you

For the love I have for you none can understand

It cannot be duplicated or fashioned by anything
made by mankind

They may search for it on the highest mountains
They may look for it in the lowest valleys
But it would be a fruitless search that ends with
nothing

No one can steal my love or borrow it or save it
Or copy it or crush it or buy it

No one can love you the way I love you
Because this love is from someone god created
just to love you

Alexander Michaels

All I See Is You

The wind brushes across my face,
and I look up at the clouds and all I see is you

My feet feel strange as I walk,
and as I look at the ground all I feel is you

My heart starts beating faster,
and as I put my hand to my chest the heart I feel is
yours

I close my eyes in wonder,
and the image I see is one of yours

I open my eyes in anticipation,
and there you are just there waiting for me

And your smile is all it takes to remind me,
why you have completely captivated me

You Are My Melody

You are:

The sound I hear when the birds sing by my window in the morning

The harmony I experience when I listen to the best orchestra

The feeling I get when I hear a baby laugh

The emotion I feel when I listen to beautiful poetry

The sounds I hear from you when we make love

The sound of silence and peace when all is still

Yes you are the music of my existence

Yes you are my melody

Alexander Michaels

Stillness and Gentleness

Still as the water on a quite pond

Silent as the owl that flies through the quite night

Gentle as the brush of a butterfly's wings

Smooth as the finest silk ever made

Strong as the shiny strands of a spider's web

This is how your love gently captured me

And wrapped me in a velvety softness so gentle
and yet so strong

I cannot escape

No, I will not escape

Without You I am Nothing

Without me you are nothing, I shouted in anger as you turned around and walked out the door

Without you I am nothing, I whispered to myself as you looked at me and behind you shut the door

I don't need you I said, as I threw the pillow at the door after you

Everything I have done, all the joy I remember I cry has been with you

How can I live without you I sobbed, as I put my hands to my face and felt my tears flow

I will never forgive you I thought, as I walked towards the door pulled by a force I do not know

I'll always love and never let you go I knew, as I fell into your arms when you walked back into my life.

Alexander Michaels

That Look In Your Eyes

That look in your eyes when we first made love

A look I will always remember till my dying days

The passion, the love, the gentleness, the wonder

The satisfaction, the crying, the happiness

That look in your eyes I know will never forget

*For I believe that was when you knew and truly
took me into your heart*

*And whenever I wonder and ponder how I feel
about you*

*I remember that look in your eyes and know I will
always love you*

You Captivate Me

I sit by the phone waiting for you to call

This is crazy I have just met you and yet this is
what I do

I have never felt this way about anybody, no not
ever

Like a teenager with a crush on a high school
sweetheart that needs no reason

No it cannot be true I must have just imagined
you, my feelings cannot be

There is no way I could feel this way for someone I
just met no matter who they are

The phone is ringing can it be you that is calling

My heart stops and the world stops as I listen to a
voice

Oh my soul it is you and you've completely
captivated me.

You Make Me Jealous

*Yes I am a jealous person
I was not always so but since I met you I have
become a changed and jealous one*

*Anyone that has such as you and is not jealous,
Has either not experienced your love or cannot
experience your love*

*Sure your love is so overwhelming so overflowing,
That it can probably fill the world and still not be
diminished*

*And sure I an willing to share my wealth, my time
with all who deserve it*

*And yet stubbornly I choose to remain selfish on
this one thing,*

and remain a jealous one for you

I cannot share your love must keep you all to me

Alexander Michaels

I Will Not Take You back

No I will not take you back
I cannot take you back

I think of you with him
The love you gave to him

It is easy to share something
A thing that to you means nothing

But it is hard to share something rare and as
delicate
As the love we shared which I thought none could
ever duplicate

So now I hear you want to come back to me
You wondered if I would forget that you took your
love away from me

But just like salt that has lost its saltiness
My love for you has lost its force and tenderness

I miss your love but can never remake what we
once had
For you threw it away and the pain will never
subside

You Are Special To Me

Such as you is very rare, and special indeed

You have beauty inside and out, you make me
want to scream and shout

So much power and intelligence your eyes show

So much kindness and sweetness your voice
sings

Hearing your laughter always makes my soul sing

Your encouragement makes me want to make a
go of it and succeed

I wanted to find someone who is beautiful, clever
and kind

Now that I met you I know I have found that
person, that one of a kind.

Are You Ready For This Thing

Are you ready for this thing,
That I am about to give you because it comes from
my soul

Are you ready for this gift that I am about to give
you,
It is something I have made specially and
prepared just for you

Are you ready for a present that requires nothing
other than your presence,
And your promises that you will keep it safe and
guard it with your essence

Are you ready for the love I am about to give you,
A love that is made for one person only and that
person is you

I Hate That I Love You

I hate you, she screamed at me
But I love you, her eyes pleaded with me

I can't stand you
She cried in pain

My life is empty without you
She implored as she moved closer to me

You don't even love me
She cried with her face moving ever closer to mine

Your love is all I live for
Her body said as our hips gently touched

I hate that I love you so
She breathed at me as she kissed me

I would hate to ever stop loving you
She knew as she closed her eyes and I wiped the
tears from her face

Alexander Michaels

At The End There Is You

Here I am at the end of all things
As I look back, my mind flashing back in pictures
and sounds and feelings

Every adventure I have wanted to experience,
I have experienced more so than most could ever
dream of

And in business I have exercised my will
And no person can say that I have not left a lasting
legacy

Friends I have collected across continents
And sites I have seen that have filled my mind with
wonder

Times of happiness, sadness, excitement
And life lessons that have made my soul kinder

All these pictures and feelings I remember
Because you were with me through it all, the best
parts of my life

I Wait For You

The room is crowded
And yet I see no one

People are talking and smiling and laughing
And I hear no one

I eat what is in front of me
And yet I taste nothing

As I stand there
Knowing that I am searching for something

Then you walk into the room
And my heart skips a beat, and awakens with a
"boom"

My vision is now filled with the image of you
And my eyes dare not move as I walk towards you

You smile at me
And my senses explode and overwhelm me

Now I see colors, hear people talking and feel that
I am now present,
In this party because I have been awoken and
blessed with your presence

Alexander Michaels

Just Like A Rose

Slowly the blood dripped, from my finger
Pricked by the rose thorn, and the pain lingered

In pain I flinched, and recoiled
But from my task, I will not be foiled

It is a beautiful creation, that rose
Must have it for the girl, I did choose

Just like our relationship, sometimes painful
But still I remain, true and faithful

A beautiful rose, worth fighting for
Just like your love, that I live my life for

So here is the rose, signed with my blood to you
Know my love is strong, and proved firm and true

Memories

Memories of the things that used to be
Memories of the places we used to go

Lingering images that mean so much to me
Lingering sensation that won't let me go

Makes me realize how much you meant to me
Makes me regret that I let you go

Oh what I would do if you'd come back to see
That I forgive you and truly love you so

Alexander Michaels

Look Into Me

Just for once, would you be quite
And Listen to what I have to say

Just for once, could you be silent
And try to forget all that I have said

Look into my eyes and see the words I mean
And not just respond to the sounds you hear

Look into my soul and you will see a man
And a lover that loves you so dear

I Have Found You

I did not know, it was possible
Such love existed, it's incredible

I did not know, it was achievable
To find an angel on earth, it's unfathomable

Where have you been all my life, it's unbelievable
That you've always existed, it was improbable

Now that I have found you, it's insatiable
My desire to love you, it's unquenchable

The love I have for you, it's unstoppable
The love you give to me, none's comparable

So know I love you, it's undoubtable
Together we'll be forever, it's unquestionable

Alexander Michaels

Author's Summary

I hope you have enjoyed reading this book of love poems and letters. It has been my privilege to share it with you. Please feel to write to me if any poem really resonates with you and you wish to comment. I will do my best to reply.

Alexander Michaels

Alexander Michaels

Index Of Paintings

www.ingramcontent.com/pod-product-compliance
Lightning Source LLC
Chambersburg PA
CBHW060118050426
42448CB00010B/1920